The Gunpowder Plot

5 November 1605

The Gunpowder Plot

5 November 1605

CHERRYTREE BOOKS

A Cherrytree Book

This edition published in 2008
by Cherrytree Books, part of
The Evans Publishing Group
2A Portman Mansions
Chiltern Street
London W1U 6NR

British Library Cataloguing in Publication Data
Malam, John.
  The Gunpowder Plot. - (Dates with history)
  1. Gunpowder Plot, 1603 - Juvenile literature
  1. Title
  941'.061

ISBN 9781842345368

To contact the author, send an email to:
johnmalam@aol.com

Picture credits:

Bridgeman Art Archives: 9, 10, 11, 12, 24, 26, 28, 29
Corbis: 19
Hodder Wayland Picture Library: 21
Hulton Getty: 7, 14, 16, 20, 25
Mary Evans Picture Library: 13, 15, 17, 18, 22, 23
Topham Picturepoint: 6, 8, 27

Printed in China by WKT Co. Ltd

Contents

Gunpowder, treason and plot

Every November a grand ceremony takes place in London. It is called the **State Opening of Parliament**, and it marks the start of a new year in the life of the British Government. Large crowds watch as the Queen rides in the State Coach to the Palace of Westminster, from her home at Buckingham Palace. The Palace of Westminster, also called the **Houses of Parliament**, is where MPs from England, Scotland, Wales, and Northern Ireland meet to do their work.

Queen Elizabeth II, accompanied by her husband, the Duke of Edinburgh, arrives at the Houses of Parliament.

Before the procession sets out, the Yeomen of the Guard search the cellars of the Palace of Westminster. The Yeomen, who are also called Beefeaters, are the Queen's royal bodyguards, and it is their job to protect her.

The custom of searching the Palace of Westminster dates back to what happened there during the night of 4 November 1605, when a man called **Guy Fawkes** was discovered in the building's cellars. He was hiding there with barrels of **gunpowder**, preparing to cause an explosion the next day. Fawkes wanted to kill King James I at the Opening of Parliament ceremony, but he was captured before any harm could come to the king.

Today, 400 years later, we still remember the events of this day, in rhymes such as this:

Remember, remember
The fifth of November,
*Gunpowder, **treason***
and plot.
I see no reason
Why gunpowder treason
Should ever be forgot!

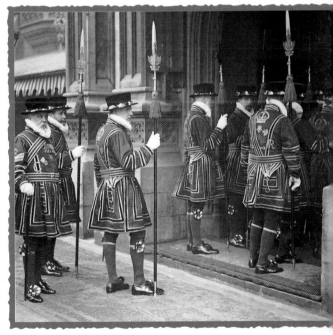

Yeomen of the Guard entering the Palace of Westminster to begin their search of the cellars.

The origins of the Gunpowder Plot

The thirteen men who were behind the Gunpowder Plot were followers of the Catholic Church. They wanted to practise their faith without fear of **persecution**, but this was not possible in England in the early 1600s. Anyone found to be a **Catholic** risked being heavily punished. Their property could be **confiscated**, they might be made to pay a fine, or they could be sent to prison. Worst of all, a person could be sentenced to death, just for being a Catholic.

It hadn't always been this way. Once, Catholics had been free to worship in England without any trouble at all –

To avoid being caught, Catholics worshipped in secret at home, or in the homes of their friends.

but that changed during the reign of Henry VIII. When Henry became king, in 1509, he was a Catholic, as were all Christians in the land. He accepted without question that the **Pope**, based in Rome, Italy, was the Supreme Head of the whole Church. When Henry asked the Pope to grant him a divorce from his first wife, Catherine of Aragon, the scene was set for one of the biggest changes in English history.

Henry VIII, King of England from 1509-1547.

The Catholic Church did not allow a married couple to divorce each other. The Pope told Henry he had to stay married to Catherine. This was unacceptable to Henry, so he decided on a ruthless solution. In 1533 he announced that his marriage to Catherine was over, and he broke away from the Pope and the Catholic Church. In 1534 Henry made himself head of the English Church.

Until Henry's death, in 1547, the English Church still followed the teachings of the Catholic faith. Services were in Latin, and prayer books were printed in Latin – a language that most people could not understand.

Under the next king, Edward VI, the move towards a new sort of church gained pace. The English Church, and others elsewhere in western Europe, refused to accept the authority and teaching of the Catholic Church. These churches were part of a religious movement known as the **Reformation**. Its aim was to reform, or change, the way the Church worked. People involved drew up notices called '**Protests**', in which they stated their beliefs. The churches that had broken away from the Catholic Church became known as **Protestant** churches, and the English Church was one of them. In 1549 Edward VI made the Catholic Mass illegal. Statues of the saints were removed from Catholic churches, and paintings were whitewashed over. The Church service was changed from Latin to English, and the first prayer book was printed in English.

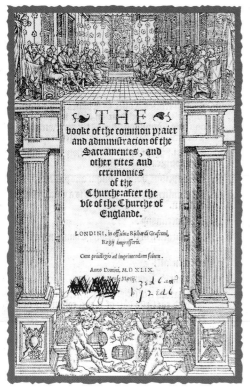

The frontispiece of the 'Book of Common Prayer', printed in the English language in 1549.

These changes angered Catholics in England. Attempts were made to restore the Catholic faith, but they all failed. Then, under Elizabeth I, the process of reform begun by her father, Henry VIII, reached new heights. In 1559, an Act of **Parliament** established her as the Supreme Governor of the Church of England, and Catholics who refused to accept the monarch as head of the Church faced execution. Despite the danger, they continued to practise their religion in secret.

Elizabeth I, Queen of England from 1558-1603.

The King must die

Queen Elizabeth I died in 1603 and a Scottish king, James, inherited the English throne. Catholics in England were pleased that James was the new monarch because they knew he had allowed people in Scotland to follow the Catholic faith. They hoped King James would protect English Catholics too. But it was not to be.

King James wanted to have power over the Church. He made this clear in January 1604, at a conference held at Hampton Court, a royal palace near London. At the conference James said he could only rule the country if the Church was under his control. And so it was that James, like Queen Elizabeth before him, persecuted English Catholics. He fined them for not going to **Church of England** church services, and he

James I, King of England from 1603-1625.

had Catholic priests put to death. It was a frightening time for English Catholics.

A few weeks after the Hampton Court conference a meeting of a very different kind was held. In May 1604, five Catholic men met in secret at a house in London. Their leader was **Robert Catesby**. With him were **Thomas Percy**, **Thomas Winter**, **John Wright**, and Guy Fawkes. Catesby had brought these men together to discuss one thing – how to kill King James and the leaders of the Government. He wanted their deaths to start an uprising in which Catholics would seize power, and return England to being a Catholic nation.

Each man swore an **oath** of secrecy, promising never to disclose what they were plotting to do.

Some of the men who plotted to kill King James.

The plot and the plotters

Catesby's plan was this: he wanted to blow up the Houses of Parliament with gunpowder, on the day of the State Opening, when King James and the country's politicians would be there. To the plotters, this violent act was seen as a means of self-defence – a way of ending the years of suffering for Catholics in England. But who were these men who dared to risk their lives for what they believed in?

Robert Catesby came from a wealthy Catholic family. As a boy he had seen his father thrown into prison for his Catholic faith. Perhaps this had made Catesby the man he was –

Robert Catesby, the leader of the Gunpowder Plot.

someone determined to take the law into his own hands.
He was a born leader, and was able to persuade others
to join him in the plot to kill the king. Catesby
recruited his cousin Thomas Winter, and his
friends John Wright, and Thomas
Percy. The fifth plotter was a soldier
– a tall, powerfully built man with
thick reddish-brown hair, a
moustache, and a bushy beard.
He was Guy Fawkes.

Born in York to Protestant
parents, Fawkes had
become a Catholic while
at school. This was
because he had Catholic
friends and he sympathised
with them, admiring the
way they stood up for their
beliefs. In his early twenties
he joined the Catholic army

Guy Fawkes was also known as 'Guido', which was the Spanish version of his name.

of King Philip of Spain, and for seven years fought against
Protestants in the Low Countries (present-day Holland
and Belgium). Fawkes became an expert in the use of
gunpowder – and it was this skill that Catesby needed if
his plot was to succeed.

Digging a tunnel

Soon after their secret meeting in May 1604, Catesby and the others set to work. At the end of May, Thomas Percy rented a house near to the Parliament building. It was to be the plotters' headquarters. Percy, pretending to be a wealthy gentleman, moved in with Guy Fawkes, who pretended to be his servant. Fawkes did not use his own name. Instead, he called himself 'John Johnson'.

The house rented by the conspirators on the banks of the River Thames.

The house had a cellar, and the plan was for the plotters to dig a tunnel from it towards the House of Lords – the part of the Parliament building in which King James would be on State Opening day. Parliament was not due to open until 7 February 1605, which gave the plotters plenty of time. During the months that followed, **Robert Keyes** joined the group, and arrangements were made to start work on the tunnel. Tools and timber posts for supporting its walls and roof were secretly taken to the house.

Early in December 1604, the tunnel was begun. By Christmas Eve it had reached the foundation walls of the House of Lords, which were three metres thick. At about the same time as the tunnellers were chipping through the stone foundations it was announced that Parliament would not open until 29 September 1605 – King James would not be in the building for another nine months!

A view of Westminster Abbey, right, and the Houses of Parliament, left, in the early 1600s.

After taking a few days off for Christmas, the plotters carried on with their tunnelling. A seventh man, **Christopher Wright**, the younger brother of John Wright, joined the team. He helped with the hard work of breaking through the foundations. Then, in February 1605, gunpowder packed into thirty-six wooden barrels was rowed across the River Thames and carefully stored inside the plotters' house.

To get this far had cost a lot of money. Robert Catesby had paid for everything – from the rent of the house to

Guy Fawkes and Robert Catesby unloading the barrels of gunpowder.

the food his men ate. Now, though, he was running out of money, so he enlisted the support of **John Grant** to help him pay for the work. At the same time, **Robert Winter**, the brother of Thomas Winter, joined the team, as did Catesby's servant, **Thomas Bates**. An eleventh man, **Ambrose Rookwood**, was also recruited. His horses were to be used by the plotters in their escape from London.

By March 1605 the plotters had bored through the foundation wall. When noises were heard coming from above, the plotters knew they were close to the House of Lords. Fawkes went to investigate the noises, and he returned with the news that they were coming from a cellar used to store coal. Above the cellar was the very hall where King James would be when he opened Parliament.

The plotters at work digging the tunnel.

Setting the trap

Had the plotters known about the cellar earlier, there would have been no need for them to dig the tunnel. It happened that the coal merchant who used the cellar was moving out, and so Thomas Percy arranged to rent it. He said he wanted to store firewood there as fuel for winter.

In the last week of March 1605, the barrels of gunpowder were moved into the cellar. Fawkes covered them over with bundles of firewood, making sure they were completely out of sight. The barrels contained around

a Piece of good underplot

Guy Fawkes positioning the barrels of gunpowder in the cellar.

2,500 kg of gunpowder – about five times the amount needed to demolish the building. The trap was set.

It was dangerous for the plotters to stay in London, so they scattered. Fawkes returned to the Low Countries, Catesby and Percy went to the city of Bath. The others went to their homes, waiting for State Opening day to arrive. Catesby used the time to rally more support, and he recruited two more men to join him, **Sir Everard Digby** and **Francis Tresham**. There were now 13 men involved in the plot to kill King James.

In July a new date was announced for the opening of Parliament – the ceremony would take place on 5 November.

A view of the inside of Parliament in the early 1600s.

Fawkes is arrested

Ten days before Parliament was due to open, a mysterious letter was delivered to Lord Monteagle, a Catholic lord. The letter was not signed. It warned Lord Monteagle not to attend the State Opening ceremony. It said Parliament would receive 'a terrible blow' on that day. Lord Monteagle gave the letter to Robert Cecil, the Secretary of State, who showed it to King James.

News of the letter reached the plotters. At first they thought one of their own men – Francis Tresham – had

WHICH LED TO THE DISCOVERY OF THE GUNPOWDER PLOT.

To this day, no one knows who wrote the mysterious letter to Lord Monteagle.

betrayed them. Tresham convinced the others he had not sent the letter. When the coal cellar was not searched, they thought the plot was still a secret. It was decided to carry on, and Fawkes took up position in the cellar, ready to set light to the powder trail that would ignite the barrels of gunpowder.

Guy Fawkes is caught red-handed in the cellars of the Houses of Parliament.

However, unknown to the plotters, and because he was worried after learning about the letter to Lord Monteagle, King James had issued orders that a search be made of the building on 4 November, the day before his arrival there. And so, as midnight approached, Sir Thomas Knyvet and a group of guards entered the cellar, where they found Guy Fawkes, dressed in riding clothes as if about to leave in a hurry. It all seemed very suspicious to the king's men, who, on moving the bundles of firewood, discovered the gunpowder. Fawkes was searched, and found to be carrying matches. When asked who he was he gave the false name of 'John Johnson'. Fawkes was arrested, and was taken away to be questioned.

Search for the plotters

Immediately after his arrest, Fawkes was taken to King James, who asked: *'Why would you have fired the powder?'* Fawkes replied: *'To blow the Scottish beggars back to their native mountains!'*

Fawkes was sent to the **Tower of London**, where, over the course of the next three days, he was tortured – possibly by being stretched on the **rack** until his arms and legs were pulled out of their sockets. On 7 November he could stand the pain no more, and confessed. He told his torturers who he really was, and that there were only four others involved in the plot.

Guy Fawkes before King James immediately after his arrest.

The other plotters had fled from London as soon as they found out that Fawkes had been arrested. The search was soon on to track them down. The trail led to Holbeche House, near the village of Wall Heath, Staffordshire. It was the home of the Littleton family, who were Catholics. The plotters sheltered there, but on 8 November the house was surrounded by the king's men. In the fight that followed Robert Catesby, Thomas Percy, and John and Christopher Wright were shot dead. The other plotters escaped, but they too were tracked down and arrested – as were many other Catholics suspected of helping them. All of the men were sent to the Tower of London, where they were tortured. Francis Tresham died while in the Tower.

Guy Fawkes and some of the other plotters were most probably stretched on a rack, like this one.

Trial and execution

The eight surviving plotters were tried for high treason on 27 January 1606. Despite saying they were innocent of any crime, all were found guilty and sentenced to death. Three days later, Sir Everard Digby, Robert Winter, John Grant, and Thomas Bates were executed in St Paul's Churchyard, London. The next day, 31 January, Thomas Winter, Ambrose Rookwood, Robert Keyes, and Guy Fawkes were executed. They died in the Old Palace Yard at Westminster, close to the Parliament building they had wanted to blow up.

The execution of the Gunpowder Plotters.

All eight men were hanged until almost dead, cut down from the gallows, disembowelled, beheaded, then cut into quarters. This was how **traitors** were executed. The bodies of the four men who had died at Holbeche House were taken from their graves, and their heads were cut off and sent to London. The severed heads and other body parts were impaled on spikes and displayed for all to see at various places in London. It was a grisly sight, designed to show that the plotters had died, and that the same fate would await anyone else who dared to harm the king.

Soon after the executions of the plotters the Government ruled that 5 November should be 'a day of thanksgiving'. Ever since then, the day has been known as Bonfire Night or Guy Fawkes Day. It is a time when effigies of Guy Fawkes – known as '**guys**' – are burned on bonfires all over Britain. The Gunpowder Plot had been thwarted, but it was not to be forgotten.

Modern day Bonfire Night celebrations.

Timeline

1603   *24 March:* James VI of Scotland becomes James I, King of England.

1604   *14, 16 and 18 January:* Hampton Court conference – Catholics are still to be persecuted.

1604   *22 February:* Catholic priests are ordered out of England.

1604   *May:* Five plotters take an oath to blow up Parliament and kill King James.

1604   *26 May:* The plotters rent a house next to the House of Lords.

1604   *11 December:* The plotters begin digging a tunnel towards the House of Lords.

The lantern said to have been used by Fawkes on the night of his arrest.

1605	*18 January:* After stopping for Christmas, work continues on the tunnel.
1605	*March:* The plotters rent a coal cellar under the House of Lords. They stop digging the tunnel.
1605	*26 October:* Lord Monteagle receives an anonymous letter warning him not to attend the State Opening of Parliament.
1605	*4 November:* Guy Fawkes is discovered in the coal cellar, and is arrested.
1605	*5 November:* The rest of the plotters flee London.
1605	*8 November:* At Holbeche House, Staffordshire, a gunfight kills four of the plotters (Catesby, Percy, John and Christopher Wright).
1606	*27 January:* The surviving plotters are put on trial.
1606	*30 January:* Digby, Robert Winter, Grant and Bates are executed.
1606	*31 January:* Thomas Winter, Rookwood, Keyes and Fawkes are executed.

Guy Fawkes' signature, before and after being tortured. He signed himself 'Guido'.

Glossary

betrayed The handing over (for example, of a person) to an enemy.

Catholic Short for Roman Catholic. A person who believes the Pope is the head of the Christian Church.

Church of England The English branch of the Christian Church, with the monarch at its head.

confiscated Taken away. A person's property can be confiscated as a punishment.

gunpowder An explosive black powder.

guys Figures in the form of men, representing Guy Fawkes, burnt on the night of 5 November.

Houses of Parliament The meeting place in London of the British Parliament, consisting of the House of Commons and the House of Lords.

oath A solemn promise.

Parliament An assembly of elected officials that make the laws of a country. From a French word 'parler' meaning 'to speak'.

persecution The continual mistreatment of a person, in particular when due to their race or religion.

Pope The head of the Roman Catholic Church, based in the Vatican City, Rome.

Protest A notice drawn up by people calling for reforms, or changes, to the Catholic Church.

Protestant A member of any Christian Church that separated from the Roman Catholic Church at the time of the Reformation.

rack An instrument of torture on which a person was stretched by their arms and legs.

Reformation A religious movement in the 1500s to reform the Roman Catholic Church, resulting in the establishment of the Protestant Church.

State Opening of Parliament The ceremony at which the British monarch opens Parliament.

Tower of London A royal fortress in London, once used as a prison for the most dangerous prisoners.

traitors People who betray their country.

treason The act of betraying your country, especially by trying to overthrow the monarch or the government.

Who's Who? – The 13 Plotters

Thomas Bates (date of birth not known; executed 1606) Servant of Robert Catesby.

Robert Catesby (born 1573; shot dead 1605) Leader of the plot.

Sir Everard Digby (born c.1576; executed 1606) Provided horses and men in the expected uprising after the death of King James.

Guy Fawkes (born 1570; executed 1606) Put in charge of lighting the powder trail.

John Grant (born c.1575; executed 1606) Was to provide weapons and horses in the expected uprising after the death of King James.

Robert Keyes (born about 1565; executed 1606) In charge of the gunpowder while it was in storage.

Thomas Percy (born 1563; shot dead 1605) Second-in-command to Catesby.

Ambrose Rookwood (born c.1578; executed 1606) Was to take news to Catesby of the death of King James.

Francis Tresham (born c.1567; died 1605 while under arrest) Tried to postpone the plot.

Robert Winter (born c.1565; executed 1606) Provided money.

Thomas Winter (born 1571; executed 1606) With John Wright, told Fawkes about the plot.

Christopher Wright (born 1570; shot dead 1605) Brought in to help dig the tunnel.

John Wright (born 1568; shot dead 1605) With Thomas Winter, told Fawkes about the plot.

Index